The activities

- The activities in this book are designed to show whether your children are 'ready' to read or are ready for a more difficult reading level. Their wish to read is the best sign of readiness.
- Many skills are involved, but most of them will be mastered unconsciously, just as your children learned to talk without direct teaching. They do not have to be equally good at, for instance, seeing letters distinctly, drawing, copying or telling a story. Success in particular activities should help you to find their strong points.
- The chart on page 32 details some of the skills and the ways these are linked with progress in learning to read.

The stories at Level 6

- Although the stories are still short, the language is a good deal more complex at this level. There are more varied adjectives and adverbs, as well as phrases which express humour, atmosphere and character, rather than just telling the 'plot' of the story. Some of these less obvious points may not be fully understood by the child. This does not matter, as it is the feeling of the whole story which is important, rather than individual parts.
- After reading the story, encourage your children to tell you in their own words what happened. Discuss the different characters and find out which ones your children most identified with and liked best, or which characters they most disliked, or thought were the funniest, or the most evil, or the naughtiest, etc. Your

ch
cl
a
c
p
t
suggesting is
happening. Do not hurry on to the next book.

- You may feel that your child is memorising the words rather than 'decoding' them. This is fine; the activities at the end of the book will help develop gradual awareness of the patterns of individual words and letter formations. Your child should make some attempt, however, to read new words independently. If your child is successful with a word that hasn't been met before, you should give plenty of praise.
- If a particular word is causing a problem, supply it, so that the flow of the story is kept going. Mistakes will be made, but this is a good sign, because it shows that your child is willing to try. Above all don't stop the reading in mid-stream to correct any mistakes. Wait until the end of a page or so, and then say 'Let's look at that bit again' and read it yourself, perhaps pointing out the words that were mistaken. Link the reading of several stories by pointing out the same words when they re-occur in a new story. Also point out labels, notices, signs etc. which they can see in everyday life.
- Remember it is totally wrong to think that learning to read always means going on to more and more difficult books. Encourage your child to keep

reading books from the earlier levels, and so build up confidence in tackling books alone. Get your children library tickets and encourage them to make their personal choice of the books they want to read – these will be mainly picture books which can be 'read' easily with great pleasure and satisfaction.

The activities at Level 6

- All the activities are now intended for your child to do alone, although your interest and participation are always valuable. Some activities will involve writing. If there are any difficulties here, get your children to tell you what they want to write. Then you write it down first, so that it can be copied and read back by the children. Make the point that somebody's *writing* is intended to be *read*, just the same as a printed book is *writing* to be *read*.

- Some of the activities require reasoning, which may need help from you. For example, the difference between what is 'true' and 'not true' may need clarifying. Don't worry if this proves a problem, as reasoning is more difficult than the straight reading of a story. Say what *you* think; it is very important that your child should approach reading in an active and questioning way, and thereby learning that there are very few completely right or completely wrong answers.

- Your children might like to build up a 'Book of things I have done from my stories'. This would give a sense of achievement and permanence, as well as enabling you to keep a check on their development and what has been done.

- When all the activities have been done, encourage your child to read the story again before you move on to another book.

Clever Robot!

by Helen Arnold

Illustrated by Tony Kenyon

A Piccolo Original
In association with Macmillan Education

Tony was looking at a book about robots.
"This book says that robots
are good at doing sums," he said.
"Oh good!" said Papa.
"Can he add up our scores?"

"I think so," said Tony. "Let's try."
"I've got 14 and 6 and 10 and 2," said Papa.
"And I've got 4 and 5 and 11 and 3," said Anna.
"Who won, Robby?"

Tony turned the knob on Robby's head.
"Whirtle-tirtle, whirtle-tirtle. Whirr,"
said Robby Robot.
Then he said, "Papa has 32.
Anna has 23. Papa has won."
"Great!" said Papa.

Tony turned the knob again.
"Today is July 26th," he said.
"We go on holiday on August 9th.
How many days before we go
on holiday, Robby?" he asked.

"Whirtle-tirtle, whirtle-tirtle. Whirr,"
said Robby Robot.
Then he said, "Fourteen days exactly.
Two weeks."
"Good," said Papa.
"Too long," said Anna.

Mama and Anna took Robby
to the supermarket.
Robby waited to add up the sums.
They could not take him inside
the supermarket because he might
eat all the tins and boxes.

Anna put everything out for the lady to add up. Robby watched, and Anna called out the prices. "£1.20p, 85p, 65p, 70p and £3.60p," she said.

"Whirtle-tirtle, whirtle-tirtle. Whirr,"
said Robby Robot.
"The total is £7 exactly."
Robby had been quicker than the lady.
"Well!" she said. "What a clever robot."

"I've got a £10 note," said Mama.
"How much change shall I get, Robby?"
Anna turned the knob on his head.
Robby did not answer for a long time.
Then "Quirdle-mirdle, huckle-shuckle,"
was all he said.

The lady smiled.
"So he can't do everything," she said.
"He can't do taking away.
He's not such a clever robot after all."
She took some money from her till.
"Here you are," she said.
"£3 change."

"I don't know what's the matter with you Robby," said Mama.
"You can do taking away sums perfectly well."
"Perhaps I didn't turn the knob the right way," said Anna.
"Taking away is different from adding up."

So at home Anna tried turning the knob the other way.

"Whirtle-tirtle, whirtle-tirtle. Whirr," said Robby Robot.

"£3, £3, £3, £3," he said.

"Too late, Robby," said Mama.

"But he is still a clever robot," said Anna.

Things to talk about

1. Do you play any games that have scores to be added up?
   What games are they?
   Would a robot help you add up the scores?

2. Do you think Robby was better at adding up than at taking away? Why?

Looking at pictures and words

1. Find the page where Robby added up the scores.
Can you read the numbers out aloud?

2. Which of the sentences below are true? Which are not true?
Robby could do take away sums.
Papa lost the game of pool.
The food in the supermarket cost £7.
Mama bought five things in the supermarket.

3. Look through the story again.
Find the biggest number in the story and write it down.
Find the smallest number in the story and write it down.

4. Here are some words from the story. They have lost some letters.

Can you copy them down and fill in the missing letters? The missing letter is either an a or an i

w__nn__ng   __dd__ng   __f   __ns__de

hol__d__y   __w__y   l__dy   t__k__ng

Things to do

1. Can you make up a sum for Robby to do? You will need to make sure he gets the right answer!

2. Look at these pictures:

Now can you read these sentences and fill in the missing words? The pictures will help you.

Papa and Anna played _____.

Mama bought some _____.

Tony turned the _____ on Robby's head.

Anna put the shopping into a _____.

Tony was reading a _____ about robots.

These activities and skills:	will help your children to:
Looking and remembering	hold a story in their heads, retell it in their own words.
Listening, being able to tell the difference between sounds	remember sounds in words and link spoken words with the words they see in print.
Naming things and using different words to explain or retell events	recognise different words in print, build their vocabulary and guess at the meaning of words.
Matching, seeing patterns, similarities and differences	recognise letters, see patterns within words, use the patterns to read 'new' words and split long words into syllables.
Knowing the grammatical patterns of spoken language	guess the word-order in reading.
Anticipating what is likely to happen next in a story	guess what the next sentence or event is likely to be about.
Colouring, getting control of pencils and pens, copying and spelling	produce their own writing, which will help them to understand the way English is written.
Understanding new experiences by linking them to what they already know	read with understanding and think about what they have read.
Understanding their own feelings and those of others	enjoy and respond to stories and identify with the characters.

First published 1989 by Pan Books Ltd,
Cavaye Place, London SW10 9PG

9 8 7 6 5 4 3 2 1

Editorial consultant: Donna Bailey

© Pan Books Ltd and Macmillan Publishers Ltd
1989. Text © Helen Arnold 1989

British Library Cataloguing in Publication Data
Arnold, Helen
Clever Robot.
1. English language. Readers — For children
I. Title II. Kenyon, Tony III. Series
428.6
ISBN 0–330–30682–0

Printed in Hong Kong

This book is sold subject to the condition that it shall not, by way of trade or otherwise be lent, re-sold, hired out or otherwise circulated without the publisher's prior consent in any form of binding or cover other than that in which it is published and without a similar condition including this condition being imposed on the subsequent purchaser

Whilst the advice and information in this book are believed to be true and accurate at the time of going to press, neither the author nor the publisher can accept any legal responsibility or liability for any errors or omissions that may be made